My Animal Counting Book

Illustrated by RENE CLOKE

1 dog

2 cats

3 pigs

4

squirrels

5 tortoises

6
birds

7 foxes

8 mice

9
lambs

10 ducks

11

butterflies

12

rabbits

4 tortoises

2 lettuces

6 rabbits

7 carrots

5 birds

9 bells

2 dogs

1 bone

11 mice

8 biscuits

1 pig

12 acorns

3 donkeys

3 saddles

9 frogs

4 lilies

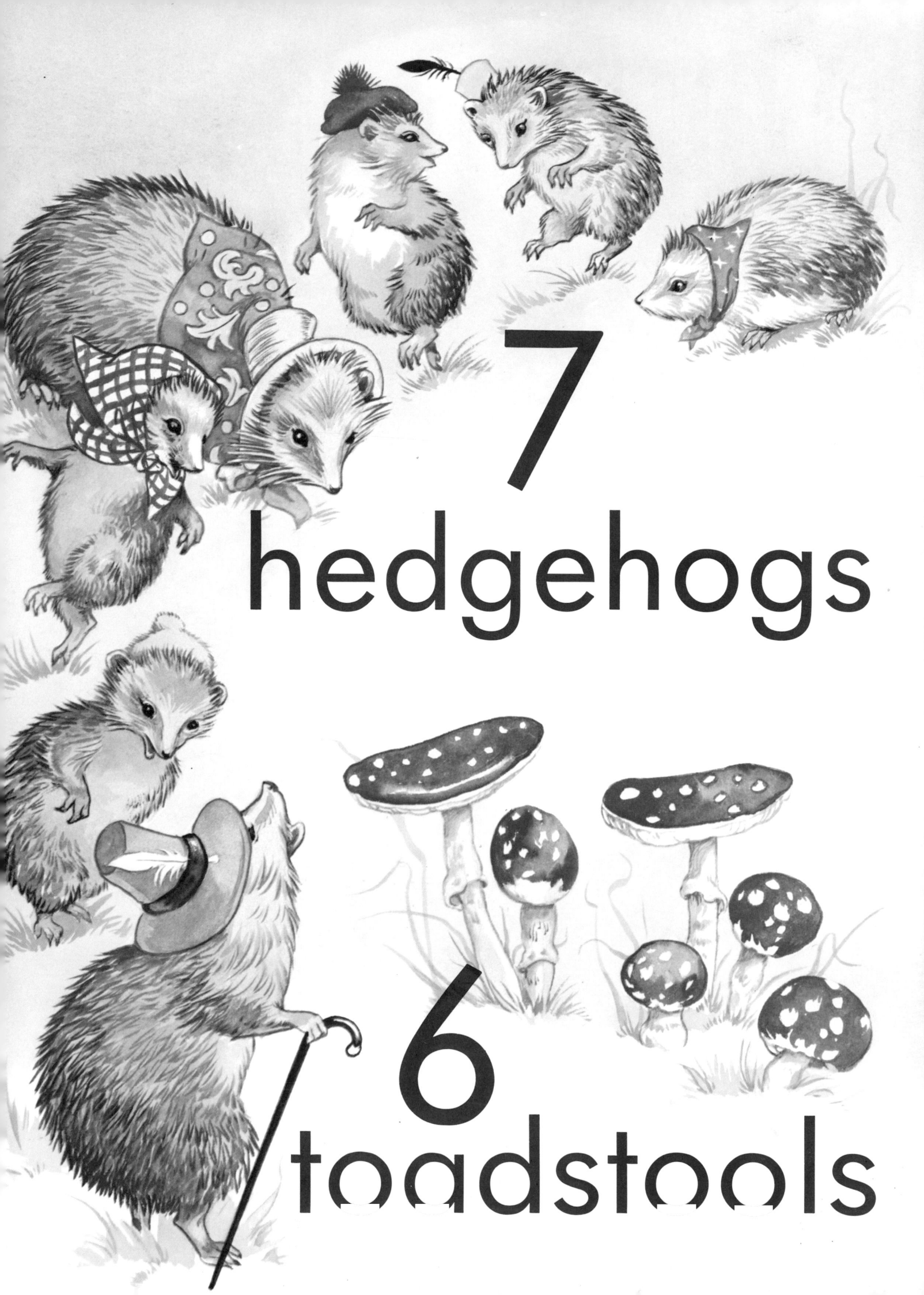

7
hedgehogs

6
toadstools

10 hamsters

12 grapes

11
nuts

8 squirrels

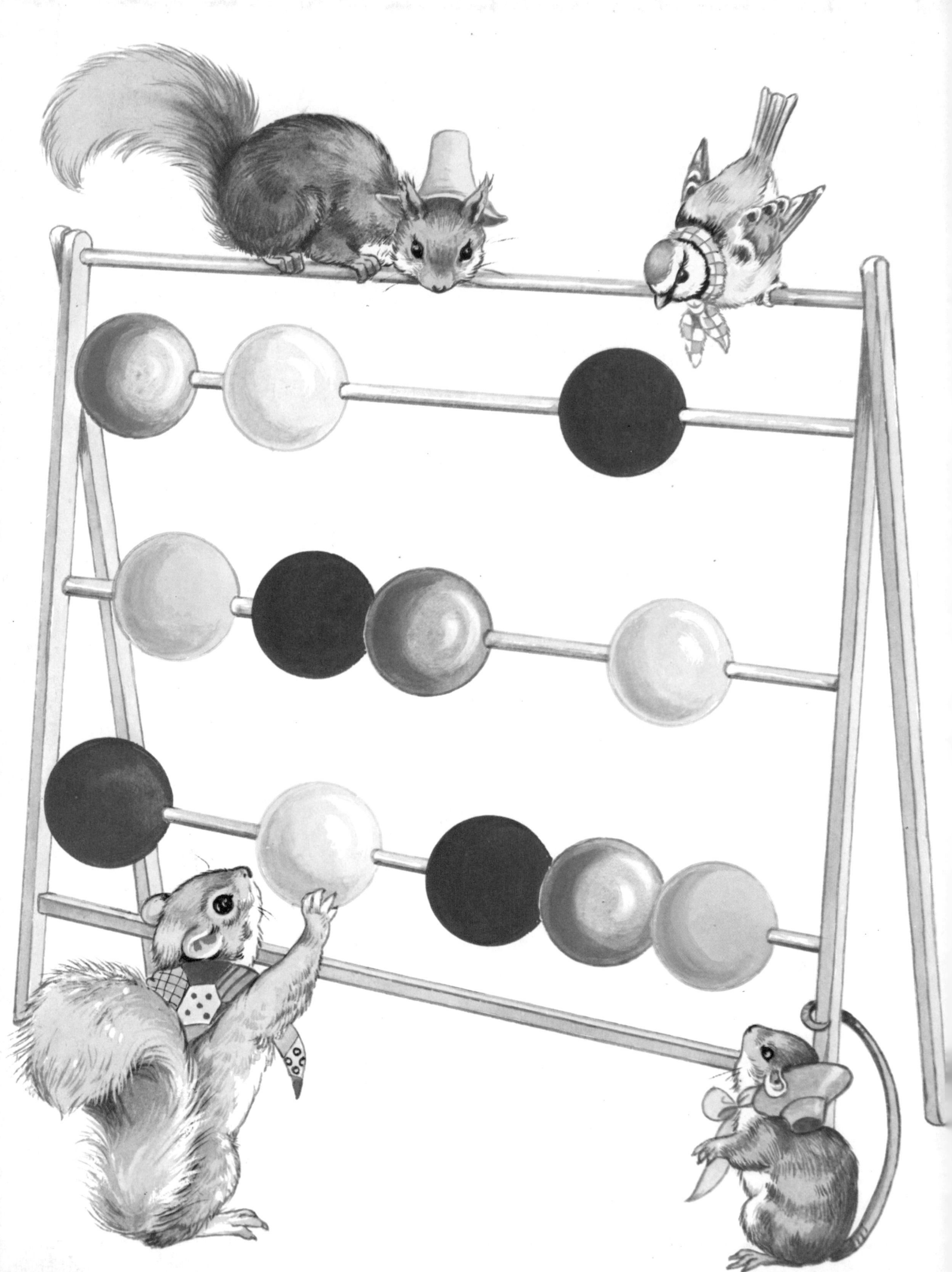